Put Beginning Readers on the Right Track with ALL ABOARD READING™

The All Aboard Reading series is especially for beginning readers. Written by noted authors and illustrated in full color, these are books that children really and truly *want* to read—books to excite their imagination, tickle their funny bone, expand their interests, and support their feelings. With five different reading levels, All Aboard Reading lets you choose which books are most appropriate for your children and their growing abilities.

Picture Readers—for Ages 3 to 6
Picture Readers have super-simple texts, with many nouns appearing as rebus pictures. At the end of each book are 24 flash cards—on one side is the rebus picture; on the other side is the written-out word.

Pre-Level 1—for Ages 4 to 6
First Friends, First Readers have a super-simple text starring lovable recurring characters. Each book features two easy stories that will hold the attention of even the youngest reader while promoting an early sense of accomplishment.

Level 1—for Preschool through First-Grade Children
Level 1 books have very few lines per page, very large type, easy words, lots of repetition, and pictures with visual "cues" to help children figure out the words on the page.

Level 2—for First-Grade to Third-Grade Children
Level 2 books are printed in slightly smaller type than Level 1 books. The stories are more complex, but there is still lots of repetition in the text, and many pictures. The sentences are quite simple and are broken up into short lines to make reading easier.

Level 3—for Second-Grade through Third-Grade Children
Level 3 books have considerably longer texts, harder words, and more complicated sentences.

All Aboard for happy reading!

For Craig, Drew, Josh, Chris, Patt, and Dean.
My brother, brothers-in-law, and brothers in
life, who give men a good name—G.C.

For Kathy, Stephanie and Christopher who
always give support and inspiration—S.J.P.

Text copyright © 2001 by Ginjer Clarke. Illustrations copyright © 2001 by Steven James
Petruccio. All rights reserved. Published by Grosset & Dunlap, a division of Penguin Putnam
Books for Young Readers, New York. GROSSET & DUNLAP and ALL ABOARD READING
are trademarks of Penguin Putnam Inc. Published simultaneously in Canada.
Printed in the U.S.A.

Library of Congress Cataloging-in-Publication data is available.

ISBN 0-448-42588-2 (GB)   A B C D E F G H I J
ISBN 0-488-42490-8 (pbk.)   A B C D E F G H I J

ALL
ABOARD
READING™
Level 1
Preschool-Grade 1

SHARKS!

By Ginjer Clarke

Illustrated by Steven James Petruccio

Grosset & Dunlap • New York

Hawaii

It is a hot day.

A surfer waits

for a big wave.

All at once,
something bumps
his board!

Then he sees a fin.

It is a shark!

The surfer swims away.

He is safe.

But he needs

a new board!

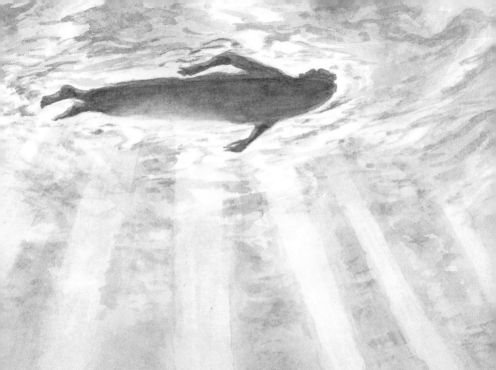

Sharks do not bite
people very often.
Surfers look like seals
to hungry sharks.
And sharks love to eat seals.

The most dangerous shark
is the great white shark.

It has a white belly.

It is very big.

Great white sharks eat seals,

fish,

turtles,

penguins,

and even other sharks.

The great white has
many rows of teeth.
Sometimes a tooth breaks.
Then a tooth from behind
takes its place.

Are all sharks dangerous?

No!

The biggest shark

is the whale shark.

It is longer than

a school bus.

The whale shark
eats only tiny fish and shrimp.
It will let a diver
go for a ride on its fins.

basking shark

These sharks
are also very big.

megamouth shark

They do not bite people.
All they eat are
tiny shrimp and animals.

Are all sharks big?

No.

Lots of sharks are small.
This shark is only
as big as a cat.
But it has sharp teeth!

cookie cutter shark

The smallest shark
is about as long as a pencil.
It lives at the bottom
of the sea.
Its eyes glow.
It can see in the dark water!

lantern shark

lemon shark

blue shark

pink goblin shark

There are about
375 kinds of sharks.
They come in many
colors and shapes.

leopard shark

This shark has spots.

This shark has eyes
on the ends
of its head.

hammerhead shark

This shark's head is
shaped like a saw.

saw shark

21

This shark
is the color of sand.
It is hard to see
on the floor of the sea.
There is fringe
all around its mouth.

wobbegong shark

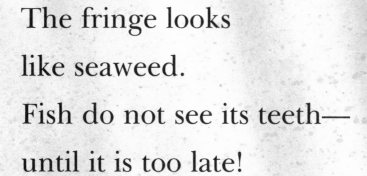

The fringe looks
like seaweed.
Fish do not see its teeth—
until it is too late!

All sharks are fish.

But they do not have bones.

Their skeleton and jaws
are made of cartilage.
(You say it like
this: car-till-lej.)
Cartilage is strong.
But it bends.
Your ears
and nose
are made
of cartilage.

Like all fish,
sharks have gills.
They breathe water
through their gills.

Like all fish,
some sharks lay eggs.
Shark eggs look
like small purses.
The baby sharks
hatch from the egg cases.

But most sharks
give birth to baby sharks.
Baby sharks are called pups.

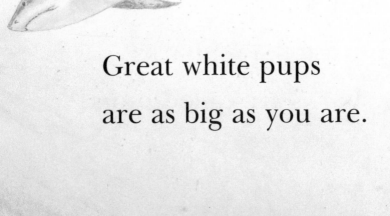

Great white pups
are as big as you are.

The mother shark
does not take care
of the baby sharks.
Right away the pups
start hunting.
They are on their own.

Sharks have been around
for a long, long time.
Before dinosaurs,
there were sharks.

Sharks will be around
for a long time
to come.